HAMSTERS
FROM HEAD TO TAIL

By Don LeChamp

Gareth Stevens
PUBLISHING

Please visit our website, www.garethstevens.com. For a free color catalog of all our high-quality books, call toll free 1-800-542-2595 or fax 1-877-542-2596.

Cataloging-in-Publication Data

Names: LeChamp, Don.
Title: Hamsters from head to tail / Don LeChamp.
Description: New York : Gareth Stevens Publishing, 2017. | Series: Animals from head to tail | Includes index.
Identifiers: ISBN 9781482445442 (pbk.) | ISBN 9781482445398 (library bound) | ISBN 9781482445275 (6 pack)
Subjects: LCSH: Hamsters–Juvenile literature.
Classification: LCC SF459.H3 L43 2017 | DDC 636.935'6–dc23

First Edition

Published in 2017 by
Gareth Stevens Publishing
111 East 14th Street, Suite 349
New York, NY 10003

Editor: Ryan Nagelhout
Designer: Katelyn E. Reynolds

Photo credits: Cover, p. 1 Niraworn Brahmakasikara/Shutterstock.com; p. 5 Gemenacom/Shutterstock.com; pp. 7, 24 (eyes) sabza/Shutterstock.com; p. 9 Meisterdragon/Shutterstock.com; p. 11 tridland/Shutterstock.com; pp. 13, 24 (whiskers) Eric Isselee/Shutterstock.com; p. 15 stock_shot/Shutterstock.com; pp. 17, 24 (teeth) hasan eroglu/Shutterstock.com; p. 19 Julia Kuznetsova/Shutterstock.com; p. 21 Nurtsani Octavia/EyeEm/ Getty Images; p. 23 AlexKalashnikov/Shutterstock.com.

Printed in the United States of America

CPSIA compliance information: Batch #CS16GS: For further information contact Gareth Stevens, New York, New York at 1-800-542-2595.

Contents

Hamsters are cute animals.

They do not see well.

Babies do not see at all!

9

Some hamsters
have red eyes.

They have hairs
on their noses.
These are called whiskers.

13

They have pockets
in their mouths.
They keep food there.

Their teeth grow
very fast.

17

Hamsters are very soft.
They have fur.

They are different colors.

They have very small tails!